MW01118391

Damien and the Island of Sickness

A story about Father Damien

written by Kenneth Christopher
illustrated by Judith Leo

ISBN: 0-03-049416-8
Library of Congress Catalog Card Number: 78-65510

 Winston Press   430 Oak Grove   Minneapolis, MN 55403

Joseph de Veuster was a young man who lived
in a faraway country many years ago. He worked
long hours on a farm, taking care of the cows
and sheep and plowing and planting the fields.

"Joseph, you are a good worker," his
father said one day. "But I don't think
farming is the best life for you. You can

choose what you want to do. Would you like
to buy and sell oats and wheat, like me?"

"I don't know, Father," said Joseph.
"I'll try it."

"Fine," said his father. "If you are
successful, you can earn money and have a
big house to live in."

But Joseph wasn't sure he wanted to be a merchant like his father. He kept thinking of his older brother, Pamphile, who was training to be a missionary.

How exciting it would be to go to distant parts of the world to tell people about Jesus! At last Joseph decided that he, too, would be a missionary.

At the school for missionaries, Joseph
took the name Damien. He was not as smart
as some students, but he studied hard.

Pamphile, his brother, had the honor of
being chosen to go to the Pacific islands

to work with people there. But then Pamphile became sick.

"Let me go in his place," begged Damien. "Please!"

Damien's teachers thought he was not ready, but at last they said he could go.

And so, before his schooling was even finished, Damien sailed halfway around the world to Hawaii. He would never again see his brother, Pamphile, or any of his family at home, or the town where he grew up.

But being far from home didn't make Damien sad. He enjoyed helping people. Damien told them that Jesus came to help them be happy. He said, "Jesus forgives you for any wrong things you have done. Jesus loves you."

Soon Damien had many friends in Hawaii.
They called him "Makua Kamiano," which means
"Father Damien" in Hawaiian.

Damien was a large man, and strong.
He was a good carpenter, and he built many
churches on the island of Hawaii.

He also learned to climb up and around the jagged sides of dangerous volcanoes on his way to visit his new friends.

One day the bishop told Damien and three other missionaries about an island called Molokai. People were sent there when they had an illness called leprosy. No one helped the sick people because they were afraid of getting leprosy, too. The people on Molokai lived in dirty huts without enough food or clothing.

"I need someone to take care of them," said the bishop. "But remember, whoever goes might become sick with leprosy."

Each of the four men volunteered to go. "Let me go," said Damien. "I want to help those people. And I am ready to die if I must."

The bishop chose Damien. Less than a week later, he was taken by boat to Molokai. He had no house to live in. For the first few nights, he slept under the branches of a puhala tree.

The people on Molokai were overjoyed that Damien was with them. They needed his help. They had no doctor, no churches, no police. They didn't even have any work to do to keep them busy and help them forget their troubles.

Many of the people were ill and dying of leprosy. Since no one cared for them, they had become cruel and uncaring with each other.

Damien saw that he had much to do.
He set right to work, building, nursing, teaching
his new friends, and helping them laugh again.
    One of the first things he did was to
dig a pipeline to the mountains to bring

good , clean water down to the village.

    Damien prayed with the people and read
to them from the Bible. They could see that
God loved them because they saw every day
how much Damien loved them.

Soon people in other parts of Hawaii were talking about the brave missionary who chose to help the people in the village of leprosy. Damien paid no attention to what people said. He didn't care about himself. He only cared about his people.

When the government didn't send his
village enough food to eat and clothes to
wear, Damien became angry. "You have sent
these poor, sick people here as if this were
a prison," he complained in a letter. "Now
I am telling you to give them the things they need."

Some of the saddest people on Molokai were the children who had no parents and no one to care for them. Damien built two special homes, one for boys and one for girls. The happiest times of each day were the times he spent with his new family of children, laughing and telling stories.

Each day Damien cared for the sick people, even though he knew he might catch their illness.

"You must be careful," a boy warned him one day.

Damien smiled and said, "Don't worry. Suppose the disease does get into my body. God will give me a new body in heaven."

Damien lived fourteen years on Molokai. During that time, people in all parts of the world heard about him and the sick people on the island. They sent help to Molokai. Doctors came to care for the sick, and workers came to build hospitals and houses.

Molokai was no longer a sad, cruel place. Now it was a good home where the sick people were cared for and where they cared for each other. Damien had done this wonderful thing for his people.

The Queen of Hawaii came to Molokai to
thank Damien and to give him a royal medal.
The people were proud to be visited by their

queen and happy that their friend, Damien,
was honored. They had a big celebration with
food and flowers.

At last Damien did get leprosy, as he knew
he would. After five years of sickness, he died.
But even after his death, we remember the man
who chose to help people.

A Biographical Sketch of Father Damien

Joseph de Veuster was born January 3, 1840, the seventh of eight children in the family of a middle-class Flemish grain merchant in Belgium. At the age of 18, Joseph followed his older brother into the seminary of a missionary order of priests, taking the name Damien.

In 1863, young Damien volunteered for the missions in Hawaii (then an independent kingdom). He was ordained in Honolulu the following year and spent the next eight years serving the rural missions on the large island of Hawaii. Damien was a direct and forceful person — impulsive, zealous, stubborn, quick to anger but even quicker to laugh.

Leprosy was nearly epidemic in Hawaii at that time, and Damien was fully aware of the frightening effects of this disease. Yet when his bishop asked for a priest to serve the neglected leper colony on the island of Molokai, Damien quickly volunteered.

He threw himself into the work without a thought for his own health, sharing everything — even his pipe — with the lepers. Father Damien rarely left the colony (indeed, for a time, the health authorities prohibited him from leaving).

In 1884, Damien contracted leprosy, and he lived his remaining years in constant pain. His face and body were increasingly disfigured by the disease that took his life in 1889. During these last years, Damien was acclaimed a living martyr by people in all parts of the world. As Robert Louis Stevenson said of him, "It was his part, by one act of martyrdom, to direct all men's eyes to that distressful country." And the attention Damien brought to Molokai also brought help — doctors, hospitals, and education. By the time of Damien's death, Molokai had been transformed into a model medical colony.